CHARMAINE WILSON is a world-renowned medium, praised for her psychic skill and compassion, who awoke to her gift in 1999 and began this work in 2002. Winner of Channel Seven's inaugural season of *The One*, she was also honoured as *Australian Psychic of the Year* in 2005 and *Queensland Psychic of the Year* in 2008. Charmaine tours and runs workshops around Australia throughout the year.

 Like many, Charmaine has endured great heartache. Her four-year-old daughter and her brother both died in tragic accidents, and her mother passed in late 2006. These losses deepened and made personal her understanding and empathy as a medium and bring a poignant dimension to her spiritual insight. Charmaine is dedicated to delivering accurate information and consoling wisdom from the spirit world to her audience.

The

HEALING

ART

of

SPIRIT

love & loss, life & the afterlife

CHARMAINE WILSON

Copyright © 2019 Charmaine Wilson

ISBN: 978-1-925846-58-4
Published by Vivid Publishing
A division of Fontaine Publishing Group
P.O. Box 948, Fremantle
Western Australia 6959
www.vividpublishing.com.au

A catalogue record for this
book is available from the
National Library of Australia

Hummingbird

I have chosen this intriguing and magical bird to grace the cover of this book for many reasons and all of them relate to the way I feel about healing grief.

Spiritually, the hummingbird represents joy, happiness, moving forward, seeking sweetness and being present in the now.

Everything you need to reach for to survive grief.

This tiny little bird has the ability to hover in one spot longer then any other bird and their little wings move rapidly in a figure 8 movement, the symbol for infinity, and this reminds us that we do exist beyond this present incarnation.

They hover up and down, side to side reminding us to keep moving no matter what. There is always a different way to view the the current situation.

They are constantly seeking sweetness to nourish their tiny frames and this reminds us to nourish our souls with the sweet moments of life.

The hummingbird has always been special to both my husband and I.

Both of us have had the pleasure of rescuing one and holding it in our hand for a short while.

It was an honour and such a rarity that I realised it was a gift from spirit reminding me how far I have come from my early days of grief.

Never in my wildest dreams would I have thought I would hold something so precious and dear but it happened to me.

Since that time I have related the hummingbird to joy and happiness and whenever I see one, I am transported back to that day and the joy those moments gave me.

If you see a hummingbird cross your path it is a sign from your spirit folk to stay in the present and not in the past, to remember your quest for joy and that life is eternal.

You may spy a hummingbird in nature, on a painting, in a book or across your computer screen. Either way when hummingbird visits you it is a sign that you are doing ok and to keep seeking the sweetness of life.

Just breathe

In the very early days of grief, in the first hours, days and weeks, it is important to remember to just breathe.

You may not be able to return to work for a while, and that's ok.

You may not want to eat sometimes, and that's ok.

You may not want to do anything but sit quietly and cry, and that's okay too.

This feeling you have inside—this emptiness and absolute horror—is normal.

You may feel like you are standing at the bottom of a black ocean, the noise of all the world rushing around you, as you stand absolutely still.

Just breathe.

You may feel as if you cannot sit still, like you need to do everything at once, like you need to keep busy just to keep sane.

You may feel that if you stop moving you will crumple up and never move again.

Crumple then, and remember to breathe.

It is important in these early days to understand that your heart, mind and soul need time to adjust, and this time and the way you adjust is as individual as you are.

Whenever it gets too much, just breathe and let your emotions flow however they wish.

And rest

Your life has changed dramatically, whether you knew someone was going to pass or whether it came as an absolute shock. Your life has now changed, and this in turn is taking its toll on your body, mind and soul.

In the first few days and weeks, you need to remember to rest. Allow others to take on your normal chores.

If you enter a total frenzy of doing anything you can to keep yourself busy, you will soon be emotionally and physically exhausted, and eventually rest will be forced upon you.

So be sensible and listen to your body.

You may not be able to sleep but do lie down, even if only to look at the ceiling.

If everyone around you is falling apart, and you feel overwhelmed by the weight of propping up other family members, it may be time to let them know you also need a break.

In the early days and weeks, rest is very important.

Walk to reflect

If you are able, go for a walk to escape the house and all the emotion within it.

So many people going through every possible emotion in a small place can be overwhelming and may make you feel cloudy.

Go for a walk on the beach, through the neighbourhood, or anywhere you feel safe. Walking for just fifteen minutes will help clear your mind and give you time to reflect.

Open your senses to colours, smells and sounds as you walk. Distract yourself from the heaviness in your heart however you can.

Remember to breathe deeply. This will help clear the heavy energy in your heart.

Escapes and dependencies

My heart hurts, my soul hurts! Make the pain go away.

It is natural to want to numb yourself in the early weeks after a passing. You may want to drink too much or eat too much, you may smoke too many cigarettes or participate in illegal substances. These are normal responses in our society.

Indulging too deeply in these escape methods may sink you further into depression and may also cause friction with your family.

Your medical practitioner may offer you sleeping pills or relaxants and these may help for a while, but it is unwise to grow too reliant on them.

When you are in deep grief you are more susceptible than ever before to relying heavily on substances to get you through, and this can be dangerous.

If you feel, at any time, that a substance is taking control of your life, seek help.

Sometimes, in our grief or depression, we cannot see the wood for the trees and may not notice how dependent on a substance we have grown. Do listen to family members or friends who express concern.

Spirit Signs: Messages from your spirit folk

In the early days of grief, you may see many signs or none at all.

If you are not seeing signs, give yourself time, and don't stress about it. This simply means your grief is too heavy for your spirit folk to reach you right now.

Others close to you may be seeing signs, but remember, everyone grieves in a different way and at a different pace. Some people are more open to signs or may have walked the path of grief before.

Accept whatever your friends and family tell you when they speak of signs they receive. Signs often arrive through other messengers and are a big hello from heaven. Your spirit folk are letting you know, however they can, that they have arrived in the land of love and can still communicate.

Body viewing

The experience of viewing the body is a double-edged sword. It may be necessary so you can understand and accept what has happened, but it can be hard to erase that image from your mind.

On balance, I feel it is one of the best ways to begin closure on the physical aspect of your loved one's life.

One thing you may notice, as many do, is that your loved one is no longer 'here'. Viewing the body will often help you realise, or begin to understand, that the spirit has left. What you are viewing now is the Earth suit.

Unfortunately, the Earth suit may not be comfortable to look at, and you may be haunted by this picture for some time to come. If this happens, transform the image in your memory, replacing it with a happier image of the person you remember.

Picture instead an image of your loved one smiling and physical, or envision something or someone else that makes you happy.

Always remember your loved one is not inside the Earth suit. They are now in spirit, and free.

Free from pain

Your spirit folk have dropped their Earth suits and no longer feel any pain associated with the way they passed.

They do not feel cold or heat, but they are still emotionally attached to those they love and they can perceive and understand what you are going through.

While they are empathetic to your grief, they are not sad. No matter how they passed.

They have a sense of time and space that we on Earth could never understand. They are surrounded by love and clarity.

All of their energy has been healed upon entering spirit and they are whole again—but in a spiritual sense rather than physical one. They receive love from the spirit realm and they are free from all pain and earthly concerns.

Riding the storm

You may feel isolated, like you have sunk to the bottom of the ocean, and this is a normal response. You may oscillate between feeling okay to totally out of control and anxious.

You may feel like you can't breathe. When this happens focus on your breath and let the tears go. Don't try and be brave.

You hurt because you love so much, and your mind, body and soul will cause you to react in ways that don't feel natural to you.

If you are able to meditate, this is a good way to quietly allow your body to ride the emotional storm.

If you cannot meditate, then sit and focus on your breath: in through the nose and out through the nose. Detach from the pain for a little while, and just breathe.

Numb and forgetful

For the first few months after the loss of someone close to you, there is a tendency to feel numb and memory loss may occur.

It's not that you can't remember, but that everything else pales into insignificance alongside your loss.

This is normal, and your memory will return in time.

Eventually, these black days will be replaced with shades of grey and then, at last, the sun will shine again.

Do not worry if you cannot remember the darkness directly after a passing. This is your mind's way of protecting you.

Focus your memory on all the joy your loved one gave to you in life.

Spirit Signs: Dream visits

Dreams are a common way for our spirit folk to let us know they are okay.

Often you might be dreaming of something totally random and they will join in, out of the blue.

You may find yourself expressing surprise in the dream such as, "What are you doing here? I thought you had died?"

Often they don't speak or smile but are simply there. This isn't ominous; it is the most common way for spirit folk to appear in dreams.

They may speak to you, and if they do, pay careful attention to the words and write these down as soon as you wake. Their words may have significance to you in times to come.

If they look very sad then they may be reflecting what they see in you, and this may mean they wish for you to smile more.

If they keep passing away again and again in your dreams, then this is inviting you to move on to the stage of acceptance.

Not every spirit is good at communicating through dreams, and you may never dream of some of your spirit folk. Again, this is normal.

Just remember, a dream is a visit and should be gratefully accepted.

Moving on

When your loved one passes suddenly and there is no chance to say goodbye, there may be words and memories that haunt us. Often we never find the answers we are looking for. Not completely. Even going to a medium will not always provide the missing links.

Some questions will be forever a mystery.

If this happens, you need to change the way you think and understand, "it is what it is."

If you are in this place, you have a choice: to focus solely on what you cannot change or discover, or to focus on your own healing and acceptance.

You see, you may never know for sure; you may never find the answers you want. Remember, time spent trying to fit together the pieces is time you could spend with family you still have—reminiscing about happier times, making beautiful new memories and hugging yourself because your loved one chose you to spend their time with, no matter how long or short that time may have been.

It is your choice what to do and how to spend your time but always remember, "it is what it is." Nothing can undo a passing.

Your loved one will still be in spirit, even if you find all the answers.

The most important thing now is to find your new normal, love the family you still have, and live life honouring the one you have lost, with full knowledge their spirit is watching over you.

Stop those thoughts

This has been very effective for me and for many of the people I work with.

When you find yourself revisiting the day the unthinkable happened and you had to say a final goodbye to your loved one, try creating a mental image of a stop sign. This may help you stop going to thoughts that make you sad.

You see it is almost impossible not to think about that moment, as many of you know. And sadly, it is also easy to dwell on it for many hours every day, but it does not do you any good.

Revisiting that memory only serves to make you sad.

If you are ready to let go of those raw and painful memories, I suggest instead only dwelling in these thoughts for a few minutes, and then put up the mental stop sign.

Change your thoughts to a happy moment shared with your loved one. It may take time and effort to achieve this, but as you do you will begin to reclaim the happiness you deserve.

This is exactly what your spirit folk wish for you to do. Change the way you think and when you do, there will be peace again.

You are not alone

It takes time to heal, but billions of people before you been where you are now, and there will be billions more after you.

Death is a part of life.

You are not being punished.

You did not do anything bad in a past life.

You are a spirit having a human experience, and one aspect of that experience is facing grief.

Remember, when someone dies, a spiritual seed for growth is planted.

If you water that seed with fear, hatred, guilt and anger, it will be akin to watering it with poison, and you may find yourself becoming bitter and angry.

If you water it with love, compassion, acceptance and gratitude, it will thrive, and you will grow wiser and more loving, and one day you will help another through the worst time of their life.

If I were in spirit...

If I were in spirit, I would like to see my loved ones living out their lives with happiness.

I would like to know I had been successful, while alive, in creating a loving and balanced environment for those I care about.

I would NOT like to look down and see those I love have stopped living simply because my life journey is over.

If I were in spirit, I would like the freedom to dance amongst the trees and the clouds as much as I dance amongst my family, as they journey on.

If I were in spirit, I would hope my people would think of me and smile because they knew me, and not cry over the one moment that took my life away.

If I were in spirit, I would never stop loving those who love me.

I am a spirit having a human experience, and I know love is eternal!

Spirit Signs: Animal friends

After someone passes, you may become aware of an insect, wild bird or animal appearing in your life.

If this creature was a favourite of the person who passed, then your loved one may be calling your attention to notice this sign.

At times, they may direct you to notice a street sign with the name of the creature on it—this too means they are communicating their closeness to you.

When they see a butterfly, dragonfly or other animal that holds relevance for you, your spirit person is able to influence the creature into your line of vision.

Should you get goosebumps at the same time, these are an extra hug to let you know the one you love is indeed close by.

Accept help

When we are hit with our first BIG dose of grief, it feels like no-one could understand how we feel.

We are incredulous that pain that deep even exists.

One of the lessons of grief is to remember we grieve because we love, and it is love that will pull us through.

It is important now to accept help from those around us who sincerely want to help.

Be careful not to close off from others, because isolated grief is a lonely place.

Remember many have felt how you now feel, and there are others experiencing the same loss as you, at the same time. But we all tend to grieve a little differently.

Do not judge how others react.

You are not alone in this deep despair. Many of us have walked this path. No matter how much you believe you will never feel normal again, trust me, with time you will heal, and you will smile again.

You will find a new normal.

You just need to know when that time is right for you. Move through this grief and let it go, day by day.

The sun will shine again. And when you finally accept your loved one as spirit, you will begin to feel their presence in your life again.

See the gift

There was a time when I blamed everyone for my misfortunes, and I was a very angry woman.

I blamed the Universe for taking my loved ones away, and I blamed others for my bad choices.

One day, I understood it was not the Universe's fault that my loved ones had passed away; it was just their time.

It seemed I had not had long enough with them. It seemed unfair. But my guides told me, "Look at all the memories and strengths you have now because they were in your life."

This is when my life changed, when I realised my loved one's Life was a Gift they had allowed me to share, and there were millions of moments to be remembered with love.

This was the day I stopped letting their death cripple me, and instead I chose to let their LIFE inspire me.

Let go of guilt

On a spiritual level, death is one of the greatest tests there is.

There are often feelings of guilt, regardless of the cause of death.

You could waste years of your life reviewing all you missed, all you did or didn't do, all the what ifs and maybes. But the truth is: you are where you are, and whatever happened in your relationship with your loved one remains unchanged.

No amount of wishing or kicking yourself will change it.

Now it's time to focus on the good instead.

The pain you feel is because of the great love you shared, and this comes from both sides of the veil.

You may be too numb to feel the love being sent to you by your loved one now, but in time you will.

If you need to say sorry, just say it. They can hear you.

And forgive yourself for whatever failings you remember.

This is what they want you to do.

The first grief

The first time we feel grief, no matter who it is for, will be extremely hard to bear.

The first loss is often a much-loved grandparent. Although this is natural, you begin to realise your own mortality. Questions such as, "Where do we go after death?" may plague your thoughts night and day.

Others of us may lose a sibling or parent quite young. And this can cause an imbalance in the family, creating problems for years to come.

Just remember, wherever you are on your journey, be compassionate to all who are grieving and feeling their mortality for the first time.

You may have lost more of your loved ones, but now you can become the teacher and guide others gently.

Those of us who have lost more should be wise and caring—and never dismissive.

Spirit Signs:
The gift of music

Music is one of the most common signs from heaven. And I believe it is orchestrated in the following ways:

1. You get in your car and, for some reason, you decide to turn on the radio. Within minutes, a song you shared with your loved one begins to play.

My theory: These days, the entire program for each radio station can be viewed via a computer screen. I feel your loved ones know which radio station you are most likely to tune into and they can see what songs are coming up, so they whisper to your subconscious mind to turn on the radio. Even if it's not your habit, you may find yourself reaching for the switch and hearing a familiar or aptly-worded song.

2. You find yourself in a department store you had no intention of visiting. You are looking at things your loved one would have liked when the shop's music flares more loudly for a moment and it is 'the song' that means so much to you.

My theory: Once again your spirit people have full awareness of the next song simply by observing the screen on which the music is displayed. They subconsciously influence you into the shop and make you think of them. Then you find yourself led to an item they would have admired, and the song comes on. A few tissues later you gather yourself together and leave the shop.

3. You wake in the morning with a song going around and around in your head. You can only hear the words of the chorus. A bit later in the day the song seems to ring true as you encounter someone or something that makes you understand the song carried a message.

My theory: The spirit world loves music and knows you are about to come across a situation in which the words of this song will resonate. They want you to think about the words, which hold answers or wisdom for you. So, as you sleep, they play the song over and over in your subconscious mind. The words in the song may also relate to their understanding of how you miss them or of how you feel right now. Listen.

Reconnect with those who remain

In your deep grief, you may have been less connected with your remaining family members or children.

The fact is, your whole life has forever changed, no matter how much you wish it hadn't.

Your family has been altered, and when your numbness wears off, you may see the need to correct that imbalance.

Connecting with your children needs to happen as soon as you are able.

They, too, may have experienced a deep loss, and it may be their first big hit of grief. If you feel you have not been present, spend one-on-one time with each of them and let them know how important they are to you.

Your children may jump back into the wheel of life more quickly than you do, and it is important to let them do so.

Do not expect your children to grieve as hard as you do.

It really is okay for them to laugh and play.

This doesn't mean they feel the grief less. They are dealing with it differently, and it is preferable for them to reclaim normal activities quickly.

When grief turns to anger

Your husband or wife may also be in deep pain, and relationships can suffer greatly during times of loss.

Women tend to want to talk about their pain, and men tend to bury the pain. But not always. Regardless, it is necessary to respect others' ways of responding.

Often there is one partner who holds the other up a little, but not always. If you are just now coming out of deep grief, remember that even if your partner usually holds you up, he or she may be about to crash.

There is a tendency for deep grief to be expressed in anger and hostility toward our partners or others close to us.

If you find yourself taking your grief and anger out on others, seek help to find your balance again.

When friendships change

You may get stuck in intense grief for six months or more, and while this is understandable, you could find that friends and other family members start to avoid you.

After the funeral is over and last respects have been paid, it is normal for people to go about their own lives as if nothing had happened.

Do not be hurt by this. Understand it is your world that stopped, not theirs. And do not be envious either.

You may be hard to reach in your pain. Sometimes grief changes you so much that friends from your old life decide they are not comfortable with you anymore.

This is okay as the people who are meant to be with you will be there.

You may bond with new friends or connect more deeply with old friends who have been through a similar experience.

Remember friendship is for a reason, a season or a lifetime. Love the ones who choose to leave and remember the good times you have shared. The road of life is often complex and confusing. Keep putting one foot in front of the other.

More friendships will arrive.

Make amends

There is nothing you can do about an event or harsh words that happened in the past.

Once the moment has gone, no amount of wishing can ever undo the action or the words.

If you have regrets about a past action or event, rise above those dismal feelings and learn from it instead.

If you are able, apologise directly or write a letter to the person concerned. If they are already in spirit, apologise anyway. They can hear your thoughts and will know you are sorry.

Observe where you may have gone wrong and take steps to ensure it will not happen again.

This life is about learning, and though it is sometimes difficult, you do not have to dwell in regret nor make it harder.

This is not what your spirit folk want. They understand it usually takes two to argue and readily accept their part in any disagreement you may have had.

Spirit Signs: Memorable scents

Smells that remind you of your loved one are common after someone passes away. And at first you may feel you are imagining these scents.

Spirits can influence you to remember and experience a smell you identify with them, such as cigarette smoke or perfume.

You may be able to smell the scent while others in the same room cannot.

This is one of the easiest signs they can send you, and it is a beautiful way to let you know they are with you when you need them most.

Significant days

Grief is a natural process we go through after a death.

It seems we will never find happiness again. And just when we think we've recovered, an anniversary or birthday returns us to those painful feelings.

It is perfectly normal to grieve again on these significant days.

Understand, when this time is approaching, that you may feel out of sorts for a few weeks leading up to the day. You should be especially kind to yourself and others who are feeling the same way.

If you do get snappy, be quick to apologise because at these times you may not be yourself. And the last thing you want to do is hurt another.

If you are feeling down, give yourself a treat or have a few days off from your normal routine.

Remember, we grieve because we love, and love is what this life is all about.

Finding it, holding it, losing it, and finding more.

Love is what we all truly seek.

Resist or accept

This life is filled with unexpected tragedies that 'always happen to someone else'.

When one hits our home, our lives are blown apart. It's hard to think straight and hard to focus on what was previously 'a perfect life'.

Bad things do happen to good people and have done since the beginning of time.

It doesn't mean the Universe has turned against you. It just means it is your time to overcome the greatest of tests this life has to offer.

Grief—you cannot go over it, under it or around it; you must go through it. And there are two ways to do this.

With acceptance or resistance.

Naturally we resist, but one day when you realise this has been happening to others for centuries, that you are not alone, you will find acceptance.

I hope this day is close for you, and I know your spirit folk are waiting patiently for this too.

Connect to spirit

Death does not end a relationship.

When you lose a child, you do not stop being their mother or father.

You will always be their parent, no matter what. And the same is true for every other relationship you can think of.

When you believe in spirits, and actively look for signs of them, it's amazing how each relationship can continue in its own special way.

But first you need to take your focus off one word:

Death.

Because spirits, like love, cannot die. When you decide to focus on the life they lived that you shared, and the life you still have now, rather than the moment they passed into spirit, you will discover they are still here.

You have to be strong enough and determined enough to accept their physical life is over. Understand they have simply transformed to being fully in spirit.

Now it is time to connect spirit to spirit. After all, you are a spirit having a human experience and they are a spirit as well.

When you grasp this notion, your life will once again be filled with colour.

Time to smile

It is possible to recover from deep grief. However, you must be prepared to let go of the pain, though it takes time and perseverance.

It is possible to be happy after a tragic loss, but you have to choose to be happy.

Your happiness depends on your need or desire to be content again.

There is no glory or life in staying sad for someone who is no longer here. In fact, this is doing the opposite of what your loved ones would want.

As a medium, this is the main message I receive: they just want you to smile again.

Take your time, but be aware.

Remember the good

Remember all the things you did well as you reflect on your relationship with your lost loved one.

Far too often people focus on every little thing they could have done more or better.

To help heal your heart, make a conscious effort to spend time thinking about what you did right. There is so much more than what you believe you did wrong.

For one thing, you loved them and that's why you hurt so much because of this great love.

They are not thinking about what you did wrong. They are thinking about all you did right.

Remember the smiles.

Fill the hours

When we lose someone we love to spirit, it's true that time eases the pain, and in time you will get used to a new normal.

However, you must be prepared for this.

Some people do not want 'a new normal', and this is understandable. But you will never have the life you once had before your loved one passed into spirit.

Missing them is one of the hardest parts of grief, and to find happiness again, you may need to be proactive in your healing journey.

By this, I mean it's up to you to fill the hours and days you would normally spend with your loved one.

It won't be easy, and it will take effort.

Maybe you can do something close to your heart, such as volunteering, or perhaps this is a good time to change careers.

If you make changes in your life, you may soon become engrossed in your new hobby, job or friendships.

Join a gym or a yoga class, not only to meet more people but to move the grief energy through your body, and to create a spark of interest in your life.

You see, while you are busy focusing on all you have lost and how much this hurts, you are missing the signs that your spirit folk are around.

It's up to you

By actively embracing a new normal and a new life, you will start to be present again, and then you may finally begin to see the many, many signs they send.

It doesn't matter who we lost or what the relationship was, we all miss the physical presence of our loved ones. That's a fact. But how painful it is for you depends on you.

You see, if all your focus is on the pain of loss, then you will continue to feel pain.

If your focus is on filling the gaps and even on doing things you know they would want for you, in spite of your pain, you will begin to feel happiness again.

So, it's up to you—your grief healing, your pursuit of happiness—it's all up to you.

There is no cure for the loss of your loved one's physical presence. But by filling the void with new people, new hobbies, and new life, you may find the missing is less intense.

Clumsy comfort

When we first lose someone special, people around us will try hard to offer comfort.

They may say things that sound condescending and trite, especially to your grief-ravaged mind.

Understand, most people do not know how to react or what to say when their friends or relatives lose someone dear.

They try to put themselves in your shoes and to find the right things to say.

Often, they will put their foot in it.

One of the more offensive remarks can be, "They are in a better place."

The words are well-meaning, but for the newly-bereaved the only place you want your loved one is right by your side.

The people who blurt out these words are not mean or horrible; they simply do not know how to say how badly they are feeling for you.

They want to connect; they want to ease your pain; they want to be compassionate; they want the suffering to go away for you. And they are wishing they never had to say those words, or that you had never lost your loved one.

So, in your early days of grief, you may be offended by the clumsy handling of words and emotions of those affected by your loss, who wish only to give some comfort.

Forgive them anyway. At least they are here and reaching out to you.

Nothing is going to make you feel much better in the early days of grief. But try hard to read between the lines when others offer clumsy comforts.

Because whether they are also missing your loved one, or whether they are truly sorry for your loss, at least they are trying.

Choose to accept

People often say to me, "I cannot accept my loved one has passed away."

I have to respond, "Well, how are you going to change that?" And, "What choice do you really have?"

In reality, you have no choice but to accept their passing.

The day and date they passed away is never going to change.

All the wishing in the world will not bring them back embodied.

When you are ready, and your grief has subsided somewhat, you may understand and accept they are now in their spirit form—that their physical incarnation is complete.

If you are strong and can truthfully say, "I have a spirit dad/mum/daughter/son," then you will be on the road to recovery, and your eyes will be open to a whole new way of life.

When you understand they never went anywhere, they simply transformed, this is when you will reclaim your life and begin to heal.

Spirit Signs:
The language of numbers

One personal way I receive messages from my spirit folk is through numbers.

The numbers can relate to their birthday, their transition day, or maybe a favourite number, such as a house number or a jersey number.

I have found, time and again, when I am feeling low for any reason I will be bombarded with these special numbers.

You might see them on clocks, number plates, expiry dates on products, or you may look up as you are thinking of your loved one and see a significant number on a shop front or in a phone number.

Numbers are the universal language, so it makes sense the spirit world would utilise them to reach you.

The numbers I am talking about are the special ones, not the tripled ones.

These numbers mean something only to you. And if you have not thought of this before, why not ask your spirit folk to send you signs via this unique channel?

Sometimes you have to let your spirit people know what is significant to you. Then they can work at drawing your attention to these numbers when they spot them first.

I love my numbers and have always relied on them to get me through the harder times. I hope you can start to do this too.

Share your stories

You have a storybook of your life, and though it may lay unwritten, the chapters are there in your memory, ready to be shared with whoever may care to listen.

Just because the person you love may be spirit-side, you still carry the stories that joined your life with theirs. Those memories are forever yours.

There will always be the chapter when they passed away. But never ever let anyone—especially you—forget the chapters from when they were alive.

You see they are an integral part of who you are and of how your story unfolds.

It would be a shame if you stopped adding new chapters because someone in your life-story has passed away.

Live your life like they are still here.

They are!

Right here, right now.

But most importantly, their physical life connected with yours made for a unique story. Tell their story with pride and do not let their book be all about their death. After all, they had a life—celebrate it.

Children and grief

I am often asked, "How do I help my kids recover from grief?" and there is a simple answer to this. Show them you have recovered.

There is a saying, "Little Pitchers have Big ears." This means that everything you do and say, how you act and react, is being monitored by the kids around you.

If you are a happy person, they will be happy.

If you continually find fault in your life or feel sorry about it, they will too.

You are their teacher, and if you wish for them to have a healthy and balanced view of life and death, then you must find this for yourself.

Death will always happen. And if you protect your kids from this fact of life, you are not doing them any favours.

Stopping yourself from being happy, because someone you loved has passed, is teaching them that being happy after someone dies is a bad thing.

And it shouldn't be.

No matter what life throws at you—the loss of a loved one, a friendship lost, a monetary loss, a job loss or whatever—if you let it beat you down till you cannot even smile, then your students (your kids) will take this attitude into their adulthood.

So, be careful what your kids hear you say, or what you put on your Facebook page and display to the outside world.

Yes, you need to grieve, as do kids, but they also need to know via your actions that it's okay to live and laugh after loss.

You will always miss your loved ones. We all do. It's just the way it is.

If you are blessed with happy memories, relish these and laugh about them with your children.

When the tears come, remember the smiles.

Acceptance will come

In the first six months after a major loss, the world continues to spin, but it feels like you are standing still.

After the funeral, friends and relatives ease back into their own lives, lives without full-on grief; and this may hurt you. But remember, they do care. And life must go on.

Eventually, you too will find your way back to the land of the living. But being the hardest one hit, it may take a little longer.

It may feel like you have been left behind in a moment of time. And, it is true, not a minute or hour will go by without thinking of the person you have lost.

After about six months, acceptance will step in, whether you want it or not.

You may find you begin to laugh again, and that's okay!

When you are one with the present moment again, when you start to see the beauty of this world again, the most unexpected things can happen.

You will find the signs your loved one in spirit has been leaving all along.

Little things just to let you know it was never goodbye, only, "See you later."

Not coping

It's okay to admit you are not coping.

Sometimes life runs right over us, and mole hills can turn into mountains.

Sometimes it is hard to see the wood for the trees.

When this happens, it's okay to talk to someone.

If you feel down for no reason, or a million reasons, try these remedies

1. Exercise—get moving

2. Spoil yourself—with a beauty treatment or shopping

3. Stay off social media

4. Listen to upbeat music

5. Watch a comedy

6. Talk with a good friend who listens

7. Cry your heart out

8. Talk to a doctor or counsellor

9. Know it is normal to feel bad sometimes

10. Try all of the above.

You see, depression can hit us in various degrees.

It's when we ignore it that the real problems begin.

Healthy mind—Healthy life.

An open letter from spirit (your spirit person) to you

Dear (insert your name here)

I am watching you from beyond the veil and can see all you do and feel all you feel.

I see you cry and want to let you know that I am here but every time I try and get close to you, you think of me again and your eyes well up as your mind fills with the vision of my death or funeral.

Quite frankly I wish you would remember the fun we had and the many living moments we shared.

When you are laughing and smiling my joy for you is amazing and I get close again to hug you with happiness but my very nearness make you feel bad for laughing.

PLEASE KEEP LAUGHING

I gave you all the time I had to give and I hope you know I did that because of the deep love we share.

That love can never die and one day we will reunite.

I keep remembering the fun I had on earth and it was a blast but until you stop thinking about me being gone you will not be able to relive that joy with me.

I have gone nowhere, I am simply at the next level and I want to know if and how much I inspired you?

I am a little worried because my death is making you bitter and at times I barely recognise the person you once were.

I want YOU back.

My family on earth wants YOU back.

Can we have YOU back because the person who has replaced you is not the person I remember, that person laughed a lot and made me happy and they also made all our family and friends happy.

So here is something I wish for you to do, laugh about me and with me because we had such fun.

Go on the adventures we dreamed about so I can come too and don't forget to include all of our family and friends when you do.

They miss that and so do I.

I know you had to change and I hope one day soon your new normal becomes a stronger and more perfect version of you.

I know it will take time but I am yours until the end of time, eternally and gratefully.

Love Your Spirit Person

Poetry — Mum

The day you went away, the sky was clear and blue.

You closed your eyes, I opened mine, a stream of tears flowed through.

The child within me cried for you—your spirit was in full flight.

My heart near split in two that day, as sun set into night!

I felt you then, beside me strong. You wanted me to see

That you were home in heaven above, where you were meant to be.

My mum, my warrior, my lady, my friend, some days are really tough.

I know your life was a gift to me, and it wasn't quite enough.

But I will bide my time on Earth, and love you more for who you are,

My spirit mum, who loves me so, an endless shining star.

— Charmaine Wilson

Free of the past

These days, I try not to look back at the things that once made me sad.

There were times I thought I would not survive. There were times my soul felt broken and torn.

I feared I would never feel normal again.

I tried hard, over the years, to numb the pain with alcohol and drugs.

Every minute of every day, I was only a thought away from the coffins, from losing my kids, from how much the world hated me and how much I hated the world.

But then I learned, through my guides, to stop looking at the pain.

Stop looking at the sorrow.

Stop looking at those who dislike you.

Start looking at this moment in time.

Start looking at the good times.

Start hearing the laughter.

And, remember, whatever you focus on multiplies.

So, when I focused on pain, I experienced more of it.

Now I focus on joy. And I receive more joy.

I have a painful past, but I have looked at it, examined it, and I do not need to dwell on it anymore.

I am free. Free of my past and living happily in the present moment.

LIFE IS GOOD

Beyond conflict

There will be times you find yourself in conflict with family or friends. Words between you may become heated, despite all your attempts to keep the peace and back off.

Remember, some people enjoy stirring up conflict.

When you have a family member who insists on starting an argument, and you can see they want to persist, be kind, as this will confuse them.

If you cannot be kind, say nothing at all.

And I mean that!

There may be times when communicating with your family is such a challenge that it's wise to stop until later.

Always try to be kind rather than proving you are right with these family members. What you say in the heat of the moment may become fuel for arguments for years to come.

Family has and always will test us, and the only thing we can control is how we act and react to these challenges.

Though difficult, if you can look your family member in the eye during a tirade and think, "What beautiful eyes you have!" and then walk away, you have done the right thing.

Gary Zukav once wrote, "If you cannot find anything nice about a person, be thankful that the air they breathe out feeds the trees."

If you can find something positive to focus on when under attack, you will be the one who walks away peacefully.

Addiction and family

For those of you watching a loved one in the grips of any kind of addiction, there is one thing I know...

They will have to reach the bottom of the pit before they give away whatever substance is squeezing the life from them.

No matter how much you want your loved one to stop using a substance, ultimately it is their choice to stop or not.

As a parent, you must have a bottom line yourself.

Do not enable them by giving them money. If they want money for food, buy the food. If they need money for rent, pay the rent directly.

Understand that the addicted person is not the person you remember—not entirely.

They are in there somewhere but have become a shadow of themselves due to the overpowering effect of the substance they use.

The best thing to do for any addict is to be clear that you hate what the drug does to them, but you love them. Tell them you will not let them starve, but you won't give them money. And tell them, when they are ready, no matter how low they go, you will help pull them up again.

Drugs are this century's war zone—especially in Australia.

There are more suicides caused by drug use than ever before, so do not give up on your loved one.

Stand close by, but not so close you get burned yourself, and always—whenever you can—remind them how much you love them.

My heart goes out to all who struggle in this war zone.

If you are on drugs, take the time to think about the pain the drug is causing to your family and friends. Reflect on how you were without the drug and get help.

If you are a parent or friend or relative of someone in the grips of addiction, pray every night—and never give up entirely.

My mum never enabled me, but she let me know every day that she was there, and this knowing helped me in my darkest hours.

Anger — It's normal

After someone we love passes, it is common to feel anger and rage.

Even if the death is expected, most people will go through a stage of not being able to control their anger. No matter where you are or what you are doing, the littlest things can set you off.

The reason you feel this anger is that the passing was out of your control—it was not what you wanted.

You feel ripped off and perhaps as though you did something wrong, even if you know this is not true or fair.

Circumstances around the passing may leave unanswered questions, which may also frustrate you.

Family and friends may react in ways that seem unreasonable—or downright rude.

All of this combined may create a seething pool of emotions, and while it's normal to feel anger during your grieving process, it is not an emotion that is good to dwell in.

Anger can affect your blood pressure and your heart; it can also damage your relationships if you leave it unchecked for too long.

Anger — Reliving their death

Feeling angry at the way your loved one passed is most common. Especially if there are unanswered questions.

You may find yourself going back in your mind to the day it happened, picturing your interpretation of events.

Over and over, like ground hog day, you may try to unravel the whats and the whys.

There may be court cases to go through, which will drag you through the details time and again.

The autopsy report may be harsh and, once again, dredge up a moment of time that no longer exists.

Your loved one is no longer in that moment of time.

Your loved one was only in that moment of transition once. And then they were transported through the veil to the land of love.

They do not feel pain anymore. They feel love and support, with absolutely no fear.

They are no longer a part of the physical world where justification and revenge exist.

They understand you need these things to move forward as part of your healing process. But your loved one would like to be remembered for more than the moment in which they passed.

They would like to be remembered for the life they lived.

While you are continually reliving the moment they died, then they too must remember it. However, they do not put the energy into this moment that you do.

They regard it with a passing glance, and instead they send you love, and they hope you will feel the goodness they left behind.

You see, while they are free, you may not be, if you have become entrapped in the past.

Anger — At others

Anger at others while you are grieving is common.

You may be angry because they seem to get on with life a bit faster, or they seem to put less energy into their grief than you do.

They may not want to attend the court cases or to go over the death, again and again.

They may even say things like, "Let me know when you are feeling better, so we can catch up."

Everyone is entitled to grieve their own way, and everyone will find a new normal, but your new normal does not have to be an angry, bitter person.

If you are acting this way, you may notice others pull away from you or go to extreme efforts to cheer you up.

It may be time to check your anger, especially if it has been present a year or more.

It is normal to feel anger, but it is also normal to let the anger go.

If anger is distancing your remaining friends and family, then perhaps it's time to find another way.

Your friends and family do not always want to feel your pain, and that is understandable.

Yes, you have been through a lot—but who has not been touched with pain?

Do you truly feel anger is making your life easier? Do you deserve to be stuck in anger?

If you believe these things, then maybe you can also understand why your friends and family are pulling away.

Anger — Letting it go

You may never get all the answers you need, nor will you ever stop missing the people who have gone. But this does not mean your whole life should be shadowed by the anger.

Remember, you are not the only one affected by this situation, but you do have the power to modify the anger you are feeling.

Doing some physical exercise may help you expel or reduce the angry energy.

Walking, running, boxing, dancing, etc.—these would all be effective in pulling in new energy and pushing out old energy, and this will make you feel better.

Consuming bad foods and too much alcohol will only increase your anxiety, so it's wise to keep these in check too.

If you are feeling particularly angry, book in for a massage or acupuncture to lift your spirits.

Know your loved one is okay; they are safe and no longer in pain.

Being in pain on their behalf is not making the situation any better for you or anyone else, especially for your spirit folk, so go easy on yourself.

The moment of death cannot be changed. And all your anger, tears and torment will do nothing to change it; so fill your soul with love from those still here rather than pushing them away.

You deserve happiness and while you continue to stay in a moment of time that brings you anger, you will not find it.

Anger — How long?

Lastly, while it is okay to feel anger for a period of time and absolutely normal, it should not be forever.

You may think God, or the Universe, has singled you out, but they have not.

Everyone dies at the time they are meant to.

You can accept this or you can choose not to, but either way, if a person has passed and is in spirit, they are meant to be there.

Blaming people and spending years looking for answers not only takes away your time but also reduces your quality of life.

Everyone gets angry during the grieving process, but only you can determine how long you will let anger dominate your emotions.

You cannot bring back those who have passed away, but perhaps you can be calmer and more present, in honour of your loved one's return home.

Perhaps, for them, you can smile more, and one day you will begin to feel joy again. When this happens, you will start to find peace.

And after all you have been through, you deserve peace.

Spirit Signs: Sightings of your loved one

In the early days of their passing, there is another way spirits can show us they are around which is surprising.

Just after they have passed, you may see someone in public that you think is your loved one.

For a fleeting second, your eye is caught, and there they are. But when you look again, you only see a stranger.

I believe, for that split second, it is your loved one.

I believe they find a person with the same build and colouring and then transpose their image over that person for a moment.

You have to take a second look because the illusion is so effective it takes your breath away.

Ease the loss

How do you make missing your spirit folk a little easier?

Keep their memory alive. Remember all their contributions to life and tell anyone who will listen.

Talk to them with your mind. I do this a lot.

I don't always get an answer, but I know they hear me.

Find a great medium and get an annual reading. But only once a year. That way your spirit folk can tell you what they have seen.

If you go too often, you will not get a great result.

Always remember, no matter how confronting it is, that you too will one day pass, and then you will be with them again.

It could be ten days or fifty years, but you are definitely on your way to a reunion. That's a fact.

In the meantime, learn about the signs they send, and actively seek them.

They communicate differently; it's up to you to discover how. Communication is a two-way street.

You see the spirits of our loved ones are always close by. You simply need to believe.

And if you do, missing them will become a little easier.

Live in the moment

Living in the moment is much easier than you might imagine.

Many people choose to live in a time they remember with sadness, while others relive the 'glory days' and how wonderful they were.

But here lies the problem.

When you constantly compare your life with moments that have gone, or when you feel sad because of a loss you have had and relive that moment, you are doing yourself an injustice.

When you compare your days now with days of your youth, when life might have seemed so much freer and easier, you are robbing yourself of the present.

No two moments will ever be the same, but if you stop comparing your life now with past memories, you may find you enjoy these days more.

Be here now, and it may surprise you how swiftly and easily life flows when you are not chasing a youthful high.

Midlife high moments can outrank youthful ones, if you let them.

If you focus on sadder times from your life and decide that

because of these events, you have no chance of happiness, then not only are you dictating your future, but you are missing out on your present.

Life is tough, but it can be fantastic, if you allow yourself to stop chasing moments already gone, and if you allow yourself to live in the moment.

Keep memories of days gone by and loved ones who have passed in your heart, and remember you only get one shot at this life.

You deserve to have a wonderful life, so stay in the moment and embrace it.

Loss of a parent

Losing a parent is not easy, no matter where you sit in your relationship with them.

When your much-loved mother closes her eyes for the final time, this can tear you apart. The same is true for a much loved father.

When your remaining parent dies, you realise that you too will one day pass away. When this parent—the last one that has known you since you drew your first breath—takes their last breath, panic may take over.

These parents, who have been with us for our forever, shock us with their absence from our lives. This can be a hard and real grief for many.

Life has so many twirls and dips that we may not have had time to say we are sorry. Or perhaps our parents were not as loving as we needed them to be. We may believe all hope for a strong connection is now gone.

Some of us experience our parents as best friends, and the big empty place left in our heart is difficult to fill.

One thing to remember, should you find yourself in this hard place: regardless of the relationship you had, your parents gave you life intending you to live it to the fullest.

When they first laid eyes on you as a newborn, they could see all the great things they dreamed you would be.

So, if you are missing your folks, picture them at their happiest—just on the other side of the veil, doing whatever it was they loved to do in life. Understand they have completed their human role as your parent and are surrendering the keys of your life to you.

If they inspired you, take their lead, and inspire your children.

If they were less than perfect, forgive them and try very hard to be the opposite of them to those you love in your life.

This incarnation is way too short to get hung up on things you cannot change. So change your thoughts, and pay homage to your parents by living the best life you can.

Your two journeys

There are two journeys you are currently on. The first is your soul journey, and this has been going on for a long time—through different times, countries and maybe even universes.

Your soul travels with a soul group. Like acting in a variety of plays or movies, each member takes on different rolls to ensure everyone gains a full comprehension of life's possibilities. Thus your soul grows stronger and wiser during each physical incarnation.

Sometimes our soul group may be hard on us in a lifetime, but there are good reasons for this. When you return to spirit, you will find all has been exactly as it was meant to be, and if others helped your soul to grow stronger, the group will celebrate your success. Always strive to be positive.

You are also on a physical human journey, and it is easy to get bogged down by the world and even to feel beaten. But there will come a time when your soul will want you to 'wake up', and this is when you will begin seeing signs, like sequential numbers such as 111 and 333.

These signs are offered to remind you to stay in the moment, and not to keep looking back at the bad things or stressing too much about the future.

You may hear your name called—you may even hear them say, "WAKE UP."

If you hear these words, it's time to remember you have a soul purpose. And it may be time to stop being judgmental, bitter or angry, and to remember your purpose for this life was to grow and evolve.

The new normal

It is impossible to stay the same after any major loss.

When someone important goes 'back home', we first have to deal with the enormous grief and then somehow return ourselves to the land of living.

It would be easy to stop while the world keeps spinning, but the world will not allow that.

Eventually, you have to go back to work and back to life. And you may not feel like it.

Finding a new normal is not easy, but one thing to remember is that though you have lost someone special, there are others who love you.

They may expect you to bounce back to where you were before the loss, or they may understand you will be somewhat changed.

Do not become bitter and defensive after your loss. After all, everyone goes through this.

When people try and tell you they understand how you feel, consider that grief, no matter who passes, hurts everyone. Even though you may not consider their loss as great, there is no way to measure the pain caused by another's loss.

Be gracious, and do not get angry with well-meaning friends. They only want to show you kindness.

When you find your new normal, remember to include kindness.

And don't forget to show love.

Include a little patience, and remember what made your person so special.

If they were funny, add more humour to your life.

If they were gracious, adopt grace.

Your new normal should be a lot like you were, only stronger, wiser and more empathetic. But if you are not careful, the reverse can happen, and it would be a shame to make your new normal angry and bitter.

Always remember that though your loved one is not here physically, they are not far away. And they wish to see you return to life and to honouring the life they have lived.

The gift

No matter how they died, try and understand they no longer feel the pain of their passing.

They are not stuck in the way they transitioned to spirit.

They are free from pain, responsibilities and heartache.

They have completed their life cycle and are in the land of love, surrounded by love. They have gained an understanding of their life and how they affected others.

They are always close to those they love and only wish for you to accept the way they passed, as they have. They pray you understand they are not in pain or anguish anymore.

They are free from their Earth suits for now, and hope you enjoy the time you have left in this life.

Then they can enjoy your joy, smile at your smiles, laugh at your laughs, and send you love in your sadness.

Their life was a gift to you—don't ever forget that.

Love or fear?

When this life is over, and all is said in done, I believe the question we are asked on arrival at heaven's gate is:

"Did you live your life guided by love or guided by fear?"

Fear of anything can destroy the moments that make up your life, and that's okay if that's your choice.

When you are fearful of life, you focus more on the pain, the grudges, and those who have wronged you. More often than not, this creates an energy of anger, depression and general unhappiness. Eventually, it will affect your physical health as well.

However, when you choose to live a life guided by love you smile more, laugh more, create more, appreciate more, and inspire more.

Living in the element of love not only makes you sparkle but makes others look toward you as a source of joy. Anything that gives others joy can only create harmony.

Aim for love in this journey, no matter what.

Aim to make your life spectacular.

You deserve happiness.

Walk away

Letting go of habits or people that cause you confusion, pain or suspicion, even if they are family, is not a bad thing.

When the last straw breaks, it's okay to walk away.

When you allow people to walk all over you and cause you pain, you are willingly allowing them to create bad karma for themselves.

Knowing this will create bad karma for you.

If you love them, even after all that has happened, do everyone a favour and stop the bad karma by not allowing them close enough to hurt you again.

It is not easy, but when you free up time once given to those who abused you, then you have space to allow good things and good people in. This is when amazing things can happen.

You deserve good people and good times. Don't forget that.

Spirit Signs: Messages through children

Sometimes children born after that special someone passed away may voice words or sayings that your loved one used to speak.

This does not mean they are your loved one returned— you should never think that!

It simply means your loved one is chatting to your little ones to let them know they are there. For no reason other than to give you comfort.

This does not mean your child is a medium. It means your spirit person has taken the opportunity to communicate with you through a young mind that is in the moment.

Two- to four-year-olds are always in the moment. And they will repeat words (good and bad).

It's the perfect way for your spirit folk to get in touch.

Don't press your child for more and more; just accept the communication with a smile. If you press for more you will put stress on your child and they may make up things to please you.

This type of spirit communication happens often, but usually only one or two incidents for each person who has passed away.

Messages from spirits—out of the mouths of babes—is a beautiful thing. If it should happen to you, treasure this special gift and new memory from your spirit person.

Closer to spirit

If you want a closer connection to spirit, you must work for it.

It doesn't just happen.

First and foremost, you must try to relieve yourself of all negative thoughts and feelings about death and spirit.

You must realise that Earth is a school for souls to learn and evolve.

You must understand everything that has happened to you is a result of your choices or your fate.

If it was your choice, accept responsibility.

If it was fate, and you were innocent or helpless, accept the lesson that fate has planted for you to recover from.

Begin working on forgiveness of yourself and of others.

Stop blaming the world, and especially the spirit world, for your mishaps.

Meditate to learn about you.

Blocking out the world for a half an hour a day while you work on your soul is essential for gaining a closer connection to the universe.

Remember your body is your temple and treat it with respect. If you are unhealthy and you can make changes to improve this, this is most important.

The truth is, to get closer to the spirit world, you must first make firm friends with YOU.

Never forget you are a spirit having a human experience.

Full access

When you go home to spirit, you are no longer hindered by physical or emotional limitations.

In spirit, we realise our full potential and we can see, hear and feel any thoughts or events we wish to tune into.

I do not believe we miss our Earth people.

Our boundaries are limitless, there is nowhere and nothing we cannot explore.

As spirit, some of us may travel far and wide while others stay with the love.

You may become your loved one's heaven.

I do not believe we miss Earth at all.

I believe we have full access to those we love.

I believe we can learn as much as we want to, the choice is ours.

There is no reason to fear for your spirit people, they are always okay.

Now it's time for you to be okay too.

Heaven or hell

Hell is a state of mind caused by how we perceive our situation.

We visit many different levels of hell in our lifetime. Sometimes the death of a loved one feels like hell. A long illness, an accident with many complications, financial difficulties, addiction, relationship trouble etc. Each can be a kind of hell.

You see, Hell is here on Earth and is often triggered by our situation, but with the right attitude and choices, we can leave these levels of hell and once again find Heaven on Earth.

All we need to do is change our attitude towards the situation.

Even if life is hellish, always strive for heaven.

If something isn't working, we need to find another way, or to accept a little help.

No-one lives forever and life sure has a way of testing us.

Relationships will end, but this doesn't mean you won't have more relationships. Move on gracefully.

People will die, and you will miss them, but don't spend so much time focusing on missing them that you miss your own life.

Their life needs to be remembered, not just their death.

Keep their memory alive by focusing on their accomplishments.

There is only one you, one time you will be you.

Make this time count.

Approach life with passion and always keep the happy memories in your heart.

Life is falling down. Living is getting back up again.

Beyond the physical

The spirit world is completely non-physical which means physical constraints no longer apply.

No bad health due to no physical body.

No addictions due to no body.

No fears due to nothing to fear.

Spirit is the energy left over after physical life has gone.

I consider spirits communicate through telepathy.

I consider they see 'through your eyes'.

Spirits communicate in this way with each other and through mediums.

They remember the pain of how they passed in the same way you remember the pain of a toothache.

When you meet again, it will be a meeting of souls and they will transfer thoughts of love and familiarity.

You will see them as you remember them.

And once again you will feel complete.

You deserve happiness

The secret of life is to find something that makes you happy or content.

Animals, hobbies, cooking, singing, acting, painting or just being with family—what do you most love to do with your time?

I believe we spend too much time looking at the past to measure-up our present.

But change was and always will be inevitable.

Rolling with the changes and adapting as soon as possible is the only way we can stay sane.

The saddest people I meet are those who cannot get past a moment in time and who wonder obsessively why an event happened and what they did wrong.

A moment in time cannot be changed, so it is fruitless and disempowering to try, and the attempt will keep you cloaked in fear and unhappiness.

No matter what the event—a separation, a death, a job loss, a childhood trauma, a relationship breakdown—only you can grant it the power to hold you back.

You cannot change the past, but you can shape your present and your future by understanding that no amount of wishing, begging, crying, or examining will ever change what has happened.

The best thing is to realise that as a human being you deserve happiness.

It is your right.

The only one who needs to be convinced of this is you.

Happiness can be yours, but you must let go of the sadness of the past.

Focus on the good

When someone passes away, we tend to focus on every single thing we ever did wrong in that relationship.

No matter how trivial, we spend too much time worrying about things we may or may not have said or done that hurt our dearly departed.

It's madness, but we all do it, over and over again.

It's as if we need to punish ourselves, even more than we feel punished by our loved one's passing.

My advice to you is to STOP doing that now.

Instead focus on what you did right.

Focus on all the happy things you did together.

If you are not sure how your person felt about you, ask their friends and you may be delightfully surprised by the responses.

Whatever you do, make sure you start to view the positives rather than your perceived negatives.

This will help you—more than you realise—by making your reflective time a happier place to dwell, rather than in thoughts filled with fear and dread.

Perfect timing

I have long considered the question, "Was it their time to pass?"

And to me there is only one logical answer, YES!

If they were meant to survive, they would have.

There are many massive car crashes where people walk away without a scratch. And yet someone can fall off a pushbike and die.

People around Australia attempt suicide daily—approximately one attempt every three mins—but about eight a day are successful.

Some people die from breast cancer, others survive it.

If your loved one has passed to the other side, then they are meant to be there.

If not, something or someone would have intervened.

When your time on this earth is finished, you will be called home, one way or another.

Some die from Sudden Adult Death Syndrome, where there is no apparent cause of death; they simply die. Often these people are only in their late twenties to thirties.

Was it their time to pass? Yes, it was, and no matter how often you let the 'what ifs', 'buts', and 'if onlys' swirl around your mind, it will not change a thing. It will only prolong the guilt aspect of your grief.

May you realise sooner, rather than later, that there was nothing that could have prevented the death, no matter how it happened.

It is what it is, they are where they are, and if they are there, then it was their time to go.

Coming home

There is nothing quite like coming home after a long journey.

Everything feels normal and right.

I get the impression from spirit folk that passing away is like returning home after a trip.

They are back where everything is familiar, together again with all their loved ones who returned before them. It's like a big comfy chair—just a wonderful place to be.

Won't it be good when your time comes to sit in that big comfy chair and talk about the adventures you had while on Earth?

This is your life. Make it a great one, so when your time comes to sit around telling stories, they are ones of laughter, challenges, heartache and triumph.

You only have one chance to leave beautiful memories, as did those who have gone before you.

Go on, make this life great—to remember for eternity.

Choose joy

Never become so bitter you cannot feel joy.

So often life seems to take our joy away. We find ourselves starting to question everything.

When the harsh side of life decides to challenge our existence, it seems no matter how many steps we take forward, we are pushed further back.

But we are all in this together—fighting our own battles, claiming our own victories, facing our own fears and looking for something to believe in.

We all have reason to be angry, bitter, hurt or sad, but we also have every reason to be happy, grateful, dynamic and fulfilled.

Quite simply, it's down to choice. I can look back on my life and say, "It has been hard, sad, and tiring," or I can look back and say, "It has been challenging, love-filled and exciting."

Because both statements are correct. But in my heart and soul I want to feel JOY

I want to live without regret and in total gratitude for all I have had and all I do have. My family in spirit are amazing—and yes, it was hard to lose them. But my living family is just as amazing.

So today I choose JOY! I refuse to be bitter about anything. It simply makes no sense.

We grieve differently

Grief is not the same for everyone.

Some people fall into bed and stay for hours crying.

Some people get very busy and seem not to grieve at all.

Some people get irritable and push other family members away, while others shut down completely.

There is no set way to grieve. Or you may feel you have not given yourself enough time to grieve.

However, your way and time of grieving may vary from others.

Do your best, and remember no matter how uniquely you express your grief, even if less intensely than others, you have lost someone close and you are vulnerable.

You are in grief. Just let it come and go, and don't try to do as others do.

Do it your way.

Spirit Signs: The butterfly

Many people hold the symbol of the butterfly close to their hearts as a sign from spirit.

This is also a favourite amongst our spirit folk.

Perhaps our folk in the spirit realm are easily able to direct these delicate beauties in our direction and then make us think of them by standing close.

On our end, we feel our loved one's energy, so we are thinking about them when we notice their gift of love—the butterfly.

Even in seasons when butterflies are not plentiful, your spirit folk will direct your attention to pictures of butterflies. Or you may find your eye drawn to a tattoo of a butterfly and then notice your thoughts directed to the one sharing the gift.

Signs from heaven or gifts of love—either way the butterfly is certainly a favourite, in both realms.

Grief and Christmas: Part 1

Christmas without that special someone for the first time can be daunting and distressing. However, you can not only survive it but you can honour and include your missing loved one in the festivities.

Some of you may be so heartbroken that you will not even want to consider this, but read on and perhaps you will change your mind.

The first thing to think about is whether and how much your loved one enjoyed Christmas. If they did, then perhaps you could consider celebrating Christmas in their honour.

You may not feel like celebrating the whole big day, or you may not have the motivation to organize anything. But consider booking a restaurant meal for the family where you can allow yourself to be influenced in the infectious happiness of other patrons.

Or you could go to someone else's house this year and let them do the work. You deserve a rest; it has been a hard year. But do try and make the effort. You have other family members who love you and want to be with you as well.

Or leave an edible gift that was a favourite of your loved one under the tree. Enjoy a 'love feast' as the remaining family share food, drink and happy memories of your loved one. If you sit very still, you might feel your spirit folk with you.

Or buy something special to remember your loved one. For the females, consider a Pandora bead bracelet you can add to each year and that can be worn by other family members on special occasions. For the males, consider a collectable your loved one would have enjoyed. These can be handed down as family heirlooms.

Or donate a present in your loved one's name to one of the many Christmas charity appeals. Let someone not so fortunate enjoy a gift. You are not only acknowledging your loved one but you are 'paying it forward'.

Grief and Christmas: Part 2

Avoid the mad rush of shopping—it can be stressful especially when you are feeling low. Shop online or send out someone you love and trust with a list.

For the food shopping, some of the major supermarkets offer home delivery. Utilise these services to save your sanity.

As the day approaches, make sure you spoil yourself a little too. Perhaps take time to have a massage or a manicure. Go further and get your nails decorated for Christmas.

Allow the younger generation to decorate the house the way they would like.

Get into the spirit and attend a Christmas carol service. Not only will it take you back to happier days, but it will create a wonderful energy for the whole family.

Gift yourself with meditation time or some yoga. Both will help you stay in the moment of now rather than in a moment that no longer exists.

Above all, remember Christmas is a time for family, past and present. You may not feel like it, but others will.

Those who are spirit-side may have adored this day, and it would be terrible for them to see you low and unhappy on a day that once brought them such joy.

This first year will not be easy; it never is. But remember that one day you too will be on the other side looking in on your family. Imagine how you might feel if they disregarded Christmas simply because you had passed.

Yes, it is commercialized and can be a pain, but strangely it is a time we often think back on and hold dear in our memory.

Perhaps remember how Christmas felt to you as a child and ask yourself if you are creating the best possible memories for your children and grandchildren.

When we join our loved ones on the other side, all we can leave behind is memories and love, so why not make every opportunity to be with your loved ones extra special, including this Christmas.

It could be hard for you to get through Christmas this year because someone you loved, who is no longer here, once made it extra special for you.

Food for thought at Christmas.

From cradle to grave

Life comes full circle for many, not all, as some pass quickly into the realm of spirit and do not complete the whole experience.

As young babies we are watched by our parents when we sleep at night and they check anxiously to see the rise and fall of our chests.

I believe our souls are ageless and timeless, and that we experience frustration with our limitations from a young age. Many of us don't remember these frustrations and nor can babies express why they are frustrated.

I wonder how frustrated we must be when we realise we have to learn to walk and talk again.

We are dependent on others for our care as little babies, and when we reach the end of our physical existence, the process cycles around again.

Once again, we may be frustrated by our lack of mobility and how our speech begins to slur with age. One day, the very babies who we once watched over to check the rise and fall of their chests, begin watching over us to ensure we are still breathing.

When we close our eyes for the last time, we are born into the realm of spirit, greeted by all who have gone before us and who wait lovingly for our arrival.

So it is when we are born into his world as a tiny baby, greeted happily and lovingly by those who are expecting us here.

Around and around we go.

Suicide — Part 1

Suicide. The word has the power to evoke a million different responses in a million individuals and so I prefer to say, "They took themselves home."

I consider that once a person makes the decision to take their own life, they may feel a certain relief in their souls, and for this reason they may appear normal again, or even happier than they were, in the days leading up to their death.

This positive shift could ease your worry, and so you may be off-guard when the event takes place.

People who take themselves home are often chronically depressed. This may or may not be obvious to others around them. Only those who have fought depression as long they can, and are unable to see light in an endless dark tunnel, will make the choice to leave.

Not everyone seeks treatment for depression, some self-medicate.

Some try to get better, but perhaps the treatment is not effective, or it is not enough to make a difference.

If someone had diabetes or cancer and did not treat their disease correctly, or the treatment was too little or too late, the consequences would be the same, they could pass away.

So it is with depression—if it is not recognised and treated effectively, it can kill.

Like all spirits who pass away, those who 'take themselves home' cross immediately. And like all spirits who cross, I believe they also participate in a life review.

They, too, can see the effect they have had on those left behind.

In the spirit realm, they are not treated any differently than one who passed away by natural cause or by accident.

They are happy, also, to be back with those who have gone before them, and they are treated with love and happiness upon their arrival.

It is not their fault if their mind was unwell or their pain too much to bear.

Suicide — Part 2

When someone decides to take themselves home, they probably do not realise how much you care. They are in a black abyss in which all they can see is their own perceived failures or darkness.

They are not thinking of you or anyone else in that moment; they are only thinking of being free from whatever delusions their unhealthy mind has fed them, or whatever physical pain has caused them suffering.

This choice is never between you and them.

Although you may be able to string together events that appeared to be the 'straw that broke the camel's back', by no means should you lay blame for this death on anyone else—no matter how much you think another's words or actions contributed to this choice.

It is neither fair nor true to say another was the sole cause of a person's choice to die.

Usually, depression leading to suicide begins invisibly and may lie dormant for many years, compounding with each disappointment or setback.

To blame yourself or another for your loved one's death is only taking the focus off your recovery from this terrible tragedy.

Do not hate them for what they did. Do get angry for a while—if you must. But most importantly remember your loved one also loved you, and though they forgot or seemed to forget your love, they will know it now.

Keep sending them love. They can feel it. They can feel any emotion you send to them.

If someone you love has taken themselves home, you need to be very kind to yourself and to everyone else involved.

You will never know why it was that day or that moment. The only thing you will ever know for sure is that they are 'home'. And if you can have faith that 'home' or 'heaven' is a place where all our earthly worries cease to exist, then you will understand your loved one is whole again and free from suffering.

One of the most important things you can do, if someone you love has taken themselves home, is to educate yourself about depression and its causes.

Understand and accept you cannot look at someone and see what he or she is thinking. No-one ever knows exactly what lies behind another's eyes.

Stop beating yourself up by saying you should have known. Those who make the choice to take themselves home are often good at masking how they truly feel and think.

Be kind to you.

Where are they now?

Spirits do not stay where they passed away, unless it was at home and they still have people they love there.

A spirit's home is where love is, and if you are someone they love they will spend time with you and with others who loved them.

If they were murdered, they will not be stuck in the place they were taken. They will return to love.

If they should pass away in an accident, they will not stay in that place. They have no love for it; they will always be with you.

If they should pass away in hospital, they will not roam the halls—they will come to you, where love is.

No matter how and where a person passed, they will come to you—where love is!

Roadside crosses and memorials are for those still living; they hold no magnetism for the souls of those who passed there.

Graveyards are empty of spirits, except when you who grieve go to visit their graves; then your dearly departed might travel with you.

There are more spirits roaming around shopping centres and places full of people because spirit folk travel with those they love.

Spirits dwell where love is. Always and forever.

A new beginning

When you finally accept you have not lost your loved one completely, and that they travel beside you in spirit...

When you are able to stop seeing them in their coffin or sick bed...

When you start to focus on the happy times and do not dwell in moments that took their life away...

When you understand that every time you dwell on their death, they must too because they are tuned into your thoughts...

When you finally and firmly understand you are the one who is in control of your thoughts...

When that light bulb switches on, and you know your thinking has the power to make you sad or happy...

When you comprehend your loved one doesn't want you to talk only of their death...

When you start to talk instead about all the wonderful, funny and often ordinary life experiences they had...

When you finally see their life was a gift to you, and they gave you all they had to give...

That is when your life will change!

That is when you will start to be happy again!

Because, like it or not, we all have an expiry date; and one of life's secrets is to keep living, even when you feel it's too hard.

Yes, you will miss them physically, but in time, like me and others, you will feel your loved one is still around. You may even create more memories with them through the spirit signs they send.

But first, you must accept them as your spirit person.

Are you ready to accept a different but beautiful relationship with your spirit person?

It's possible—if you believe it.

Poetry —
Since you've been gone

Since you've been gone, I have traveled many miles.

I have laughed and cried, lost my way, and lost my smiles.

I have traveled and tasted foods across the world.

I have loved and hated, lived and learned.

But all these years since you've been gone, you have never left my mind for long.

A love like ours—unbreakable as steel—it's you and me, and it's more than real.

No veil nor universe, no body nor time can take the love which is yours and mine.

— Charmaine Wilson

Take care of you

Meditating only five minutes a day can help you learn to stay in the moment. If done regularly, this practice relieves anxiety and stress.

Reading books on recovering from grief or learning about spirit can help you with your sadness.

Learning to control your anger and not letting it control you is easier than you might think, but you must invest the time.

When you worry about things, assess whether your worry will change the situation or not. If not, flick the switch, and when the worry comes find something happy or reassuring to think of instead.

There is always a pleasant thought you can have—you just have to choose to think it.

Fearing things that are out of your hands does nothing good for anyone.

When we have fears about things that are out of our hands happening in the world, things we cannot change, and we spread those fears by posting memes to share our fears with others, then we are aggravating our and others' sadness and anxiety.

Be selective about what social media pages you follow; look for positive and uplifting pages.

Your body is your vehicle in life. Treat it as you would a brand-new car. You will be here as long as it takes, so you may as well have a great vehicle for the journey.

Look after you. Starting with the way you think.

Wills and estates

There is no money in the afterlife, so it ceases to be problem for those you love in spirit.

Often, after a death, there is a scramble to secure as much of the estate as everyone thinks they deserve or can get.

At times, the last will and testament is challenged, and the end result is a family in tatters.

More often than not, the only winners are the solicitors who take the case on when it goes to court.

Many bereaved ask me what their spirit folk thinks of this person or that person with regards to division of the estate, and it's usually a shoulder shrug from the other side.

Their feeling is that family, friendships and love are far more important than money.

They are aware when their will is not followed, but it matters less to them than the love they shared and the life they lived.

Money is an earth problem.

Not a heavenly one.

Time is fleeting

Time is going too fast for me. And I feel each day going quicker.

Looking back, I can hardly believe how many decades have passed since my life was turned upside down.

The angry young person I was after the death of my brother and daughter is nowhere to be seen, and time is quickening at a rate that reminds me how soon it will run out.

Each day is so special, and now I truly understand why days spent in anger over things unchangeable and people unmovable are such a waste.

The young mother who wished to die back in the eighties so she could be with her daughter is now a grandmother who hopes and prays her body will hold up until her young grandsons are grown to the full.

I have learned is that life is unpredictable and to take each day as it comes.

My only regret now is that I wasted too much time being angry over my inability to change the unchangeable.

Anger and grief robbed me of some very special times. And so I implore you to let go of any anger and sadness that might envelop you now and instead to look around at the beauty that still fills your life.

You will never be the same person you were before that special person went back to spirit, but you can take this sadness and mold it into a stronger better you.

Don't hesitate, time is fleeting.

Why me?

Reincarnation or past lives are not the reason you experience grief now.

I am not convinced that every life attracts 'bad karma', nor am I sure that we lose children or loved ones in this life because of bad karma.

In life, we will always have to face death, and it will always be painful to lose those we love.

Just because you lose a child, for example, does not mean you did something wrong in a previous life.

It means this life you are walking the path of a bereaved parent, and this is the journey you need to focus on.

Exploring past lives can be fascinating and exciting and may answer questions about people in your current life. It is often a key to finding out who is in your soul group. But I feel sure that losing children is not the result of being bad in a previous life.

I am a firm believer that we should aim to do our best in this life, no matter what lives have gone before or may come later.

If you have lost a child, then maybe you can focus your energy on how lucky you were to have them, remembering all the joy they brought you and others while they were here.

I completely understand that it never feels like enough time. But when you understand they are only a whisper away, you will begin, more often, to see the signs they send you.

When we believe they did not 'die' but rather 'transitioned', then we can begin to live our lives with peace and an inner-knowing of their continuing presence.

Yes, it will take time, but the sooner you allow the moments they lived to shape your life, rather than the moment they died, the sooner you will begin to heal.

Making stuff up

Are you guilty of MSU? Making stuff up?

Have you ever seen someone you know, said hello and then watched them either ignore you or walk on by?

Maybe someone you love hasn't picked up the phone, and in your mind you made it all about you.

Perhaps you wondered if you had done something wrong and offended them, or perhaps you became negative about this person, fearing they had cut you off.

MSU means that instead of asking the person how they are or if everything is okay, you have chosen to think the worst. Has it occurred to you this person might have a lot on their plate right now, and it is not about you at all?

It is actually about them.

Stop MSU today, and begin communicating instead.

It will save a lot of heartache and unnecessary negativity.

Just a thought.

Highs and lows

Life can overwhelm you at times, and it can feel like the whole world is hammering at your door determined to make your life miserable.

You look around, and things seem to be going smoothly for everyone else. You feel as though you really tried to be happy, and it didn't work.

It seems the universe has it in for you.

What can you do?

Remember this one thing:

After every high there will be a low, and after every low there will be a high.

It is important not to make things worse by focusing on the bad. This can trick the universe into thinking, "Oh, they want more challenges!"

Instead, focus on what's right in your world, and make this central to your thoughts.

Keep in mind, if you have had a very low period, how fantastic the high period will be when it comes.

It might seem crazy, but our thoughts can dictate our lives, so keep positive and remove yourself from the negativity in your life by witnessing your life's highs and lows as if you were an outsider.

It is when you let emotions overwhelm you that you are blinded to the solutions.

By looking at the situation with a clear head, and not focusing on the emotion, you will find the solution.

Illusion and possibility

Every door that closes, no matter how hard it slams shut, is an opportunity for a new opening.

Walking the earth after that special someone has returned to spirit may seem lonely, until you understand they walk beside you in spirit form.

After all, life is a constant stream of illusions. What seems solid is merely slowed down, and what seems real right now will one day be a memory—even you.

The difficulty of grief can blind us to the amazing possibility of spirit. If you are brave enough to stay in the present moment, and do not allow yourself to cling to the familiarity of your pain and grief for too long, you will rediscover the beauty of this earth.

When you allow yourself to feel again, you will find the gentle guidance of those you had perceived as gone.

If this world is an illusion, then anything is possible.

Believe and you will see.

Believe and you will feel.

Sibling loss

Our brothers and sisters are the people we learn from in our growing-up years.

We test our boundaries with our siblings and learn from them how to treat others through trial and error.

Some of us get on extremely well, and others not so well.

It is little wonder, when they return spirit-side, if we feel enormous guilt over childhood fights or rivalry—especially if they pass away young, or if they pass away older and we have been distant or estranged.

Understand that had roles been reversed, your sibling would likely feel the same guilt you do now.

Do not feel bad if you did not have the connection you wished for, but do remember the good times you shared.

Understand and reflect on the important things your sibling taught you about how to treat others in your peer group.

Never stop telling their children all the amusing and embarrassing stories you can remember. These happy times can take on new life as stories are passed down and laughed over for generations to come.

Your siblings can be the greatest teachers you have growing up, and from spirit-side they will continue to support you and your family.

No matter how close you were as adults, never forget those early years, and do not waste time in guilt over lack of connection. Instead, spend time developing the strongest possible bonds with the family who remain.

Ageless children

Do children keep growing in the spirit world?

This is a question I am asked a lot. Once we return to spirit, we return to soul state, which means we have no body, as such, and we have no age.

The soul is timeless and ageless.

For many years, I wrestled with the birthday of my daughter, each year trying to imagine how she would look and what she would want for her birthday.

One year, on her nineteenth birthday, I found myself in a toy store looking at the latest version of her favourite doll, and I realised that in my mind she would only ever be four-and-a-half.

I never had her as five-year-old or even a thirty-year-old.

I would only ever have the memory of my daughter as a four-and-a-half-year-old.

I asked my guides, "Will I recognise my daughter if she has grown?"

They told me, *"She is now timeless and ageless, and when you pass she will present herself to you in the way that gives you most comfort."*

Right then, I knew she would come to me as a four-year-old with pigtails, as when I cross over myself that is the little girl I long to see.

For some of you, your child may present as the grownup version you have envisioned all these years.

Your spirit child will know what will bring you the greatest comfort when you cross the veil.

They do not age in the spirit world. They are safe in the realm of love.

It's possible your baby is more evolved than you, and as short as their life was, their entire existence on Earth might have been to help you become more resilient, empathetic and wise.

I have always felt this was true for me. My daughter taught me how to grieve, fall down, get back up, and eventually find a new and happy normal.

Our children—on both sides of the veil—are our greatest teachers.

Faith and choice

There is no doubt in my mind that the spirit world exists.

I have seen far too much evidence of it at my shows, in readings for clients, and during radio readings for callers.

The people you love are now living beyond the veil where they wait for you to join them one day.

Of this I am sure.

I believe mediums are needed to convince those left behind to continue living this life wholeheartedly.

Once we give you validation, then perhaps we can also give you every reason to continue living a good life, if changed somewhat after your loved ones have put up their feet.

After all the people I have lost, and all the trouble stirred by each death, there is only one thing I want…

To taste as much of this life as I possibly can.

Time is running out to make the most of your life!

The major thing you should learn when you lose someone close is that *time* is important…

Time to dream.

Time to be with those still here.

Time to travel.

You have two choices in this life…

Happy or sad—but either way you have to live it.

You can focus on all you have or focus on all you have lost.

It's your choice.

No-one can say for certain *exactly* what it is like for spirit folk in the afterlife. What I have learned is they do not miss you because they can still see you, hear you and love you.

They miss nothing, and they don't want you to miss anything either.

Choose to *live* before time makes that choice for you.

Old hurts

Sometimes those in spirit have done or said things that hurt us so badly we continue to dwell on them.

Even after the passing, the memory still has the power to upset us.

Perhaps it is time to forgive them of the wrongdoing so we can find some peace in our own life.

We need to practice forgiveness, so we can move on.

Mediums can be doorways to the beginning of forgiveness.

A heart-felt message from a spirit can clear away a lifetime of misunderstanding.

If there is someone in spirit that hurt you or that you feel you need to forgive, forgive them anyway!

I have conducted many readings where a spirit came through saying sorry for bad behavior. It seems they were able to perceive their actions more clearly once they crossed the veil, and then, when given the chance to communicate through me, were passionate about making amends for their actions.

In a way, mediums offer some spirits a chance to say sorry and to address wrongs in the lives of those left behind.

Even if you haven't had a reading, forgive those who have hurt you. And remember what happened is now locked in a moment of time that can inflict no more pain unless you keep dwelling on it.

If someone in spirit has hurt you, ask yourself one question: "Am I a better person or parent because of this?" If you answer "yes" then you will see this person has assisted you on your journey.

If you answer "no", you may need wise counsel to help you process, understand, accept and let go of the pain you are holding inside.

How are they now?

The spirit world is a happy place.

When they communicate through a medium, they will relay how they felt during their Earth incarnation.

If they were a happy person, they will make the medium feel happy, or if grumpy, the medium will feel grumpy.

They usually relay the pain they felt in death by giving the medium pain in the affected area. If they had cancer, they will give pain where the cancer was. If they passed from a heart attack, the medium will feel heart pain, but this does not mean your loved one is feeling any pain now. Pain is physical.

There is a huge difference between being in spirit and being in a physical body.

The only reason they communicate this to the medium is to validate their identity.

For instance, if your dad was grumpy all the time on Earth, he will transfer that personality to the medium. No sense in displaying how he feels in heaven—which, just quietly, is happy and peaceful. To convince you it's him, he needs to display his Earth personality.

The soul personality and the Earth personality are usually a little different from each other. To understand this more, you need to do some reading on reincarnation and past lives.

Are they okay? Are they happy now?

The answer is yes, they are happy—free from pain and worry.

They have had their time on Earth and they understand you must have your time on Earth.

You may wonder if they are worried about events happening to you right now. While they can see them, they are not stressed for you, and nor should they be. They understand the situation you are in now is an experience you need to have.

Heaven, upstairs or the next dimension, is a place to rest between lives and to take it easy before embarking on a new one.

Their time for earthly concerns is over for now.

Connect beyond lives

It may be years before your spirit folk enter a new incarnation, but either way, their time in the afterlife is a time of reflection and preparation for the next life.

It could be hundreds of years, or it could be a few years before they have a new life. There is no way to know. No-one living is so psychic they can tell where the next incarnation will be for you or your loved ones.

However, I feel deeply that your loved ones wait for all soul mates to come home before reincarnating.

Your spirit folk are one hundred percent spirit, and though we are living in physical bodies, a percentage of us remains always connected to the spirit realm.

Mediums can connect to the soul energy that is and always will be connected to the spirit realm.

Should your loved one reincarnate before you pass, not only can a medium connect to that part of them that travels with you in spirit, but this aspect will be there to greet you when you arrive back in Heaven.

You will always be connected as soul mates and will travel many lives together. This is not the end of the great love and connection you shared physically, it is only an interval.

The first anniversary

The first anniversary of the passing of someone you love is very hard.

It may feel like ground hog day and you may hold your breath as you relive every moment, minute, hour and day that led to the events that took away your someone special, on a day that also stole a part of your heart and a portion of your soul.

Hang in there, friends, my heart is with you. From someone who has been there more times then I wanted, let me tell you the actual day may not be as hard as you thought, but the lead up is hellish.

This is a normal way to feel.

Minimise alcohol intake and be very kind to yourself around this time.

When pain strikes, just breathe and persuade your mind to recall happier times.

On the actual day, remember them with gratitude for the time you shared, and do something in their honour.

Watch a movie you enjoyed together, listen to music they loved, buy yourself a special gift for being so strong. And for a little while, sit still and let their spirit come close.

With your eyes shut, empty your mind and let them project their thoughts into you. You must be still and you must believe it will happen. Then you will feel it, see it and know it!

And always remember how lucky you were to have them in your life for as long as you did.

Their life was more than this moment of death you cannot forget. It was a million memories combined to make that person one of your most precious gifts from the Universe.

May you be peaceful.

Your choice

It all comes down to choices, or as the saying goes, 'if nothing changes—nothing changes'.

If I choose to keep looking at the past and letting it affect me, then that is where I will stay—in the past, in a moment of time that can never be changed.

It is a wise person who chooses to stay in the present moment.

So today I want you to think about your choices.

Are you holding a grudge and getting angry about it?

Are you not changing your eating habits or exercise habits, but annoyed you cannot lose weight?

Are you staying in a job you hate because you cannot be bothered to look for another?

Are you in a relationship you are unhappy with but too comfortable to move or change?

You see, these are all choices.

The only thing we have no choice in is our own birth or death.

As a child, we are at the mercy of our parents. We have

little or no choice at that time, but as an adult who has been affected by a difficult childhood, we do have a choice in how we deal with it.

Being born with a physical handicap is also out of our hands, but everything else after we become an adult is a choice.

Should accident or illness strike us down, it is unfortunate, but it is our choice how we deal with it.

You see you do get to choose the life you want. The trouble is not many realise they are exactly where they are because of the choices they have made.

Even you can choose.

Be kind

Kindness is so much easier than rudeness.

It seems these days that everyone is in such a hurry that some people forget to be kind.

Always remember, you never know what the person behind the counter is going through.

If they are a little slow or not so cheery, take a moment to be kind and smile.

Being impatient with perfect strangers may create a karmic effect you don't want.

We never know what the person in front of us is going through.

They may have just had their world turned upside down.

They may be desperate for a kind word or something to make them feel worthy.

If you smile and are kind, it may change that person's day and help give them faith in humanity once again.

Changing your state of being starts with changing your state of mind.

Choose to be kind over impatient and choose smiles over anger.

Accept responsibility

To err is human, to forgive is divine.

There is nothing wrong with making a mistake, but if you hurt someone in the process, there is something wrong if you don't accept responsibility—even if it is years later.

We have all done stupid things and it may take a while for our anger and sense of justification to simmer down. However, if at the end of the day, you realise you were just as much to blame as the other party, if not more. It is never too late to apologise for your part in the drama.

I was taught this by my guides many years ago, and after many years of not liking myself, it was one of the biggest steps I took toward self-love again.

By being honest, I was able to hold my head high and move forward.

Accepting responsibility for our mistakes is a huge step on the path of enlightenment and self-love.

Apologising for our part in any pain and hurt has the ability to heal more hearts than our own and can change the life path of another to a more positive outcome.

Accepting responsibility and making amends can only lead to empathy, love, forgiveness and compassion.

And that is a beautiful thing.

Act now

We only think we have time.

Don't hesitate or put things off—your time is not guaranteed.

Make that call.

Visit that person.

Take that trip.

Take that risk.

Live life with passion.

Today, right now.

Stop looking back in sadness and anger and look straight ahead.

Reignite your dreams—anything is possible, but don't dilly dally.

Time is not promised.

What forgiveness means to me

It means not allowing a negative event or person to affect my life anymore.

It means I will no longer spend a single moment thinking with anger or sadness about that deed or event.

I have never been apologized to for many events that shaped my life, and I don't wait for those apologies.

When I forgive someone, it means I will no longer let their wrongdoing affect my feelings, but I will never forget the facts of what they did.

Should I see that person again, I will choose either to be polite or to cross the street.

Forgiveness, to me, does not mean the relationship will ever be the same as it once was. When trust is broken, it rarely comes back.

Forgiveness, to me, means I am done thinking, crying and spending time on someone who does not deserve my attention.

Forgiveness, to me, is taking my life and thoughts back without any regret at all.

Many of you think forgiveness is letting people back into your life after they have hurt you.

That is foolish in most cases, but occasionally it might work.

Usually, when people hurt you they don't think twice about doing it again

So, forgive them and walk away with your head held high. Give your valuable time to those who deserve it.

Dare to dream

There was a time I gave up on my dreams.

There was a time when grief and this life had beaten me down so badly that I did not dare to dream. And every time I went to accomplish a dream it would end in some sort of financial drama.

Then, one day, I sought advice from a wise man who always did what he wanted and who lived without fear.

I asked, "Why do you have all these nice things and go to all those fantastic places? You are so lucky."

He turned to me and simply stated, "Because I deserve good things."

I admit his reply took me aback, and time stood still for a moment or two.

The words rolled around in my mind. Then I realised that every time I dared to dream it didn't work out because I did not believe I deserved to be happy.

But because of that wise man I now know I deserve good things, as do you.

As does everyone.

We all deserve good things.

It's time to believe and to start dreaming again.

You deserve happiness.

The final word — Part 1

If I had not become a medium, I do not know if my faith would be as strong as it is now. But once I became a medium, I understood without a doubt that my loved ones were close by.

I don't talk to them like I used to, but when I do readings and validate others' connections to the spirit world, I receive proof my own family is only a whisper away, just beyond the veil.

Every time I see a sign lovingly sent by my family, I smile because I know they are waiting for me, too, to return home one day.

Every time I see someone I love smiling or laughing, I feel even happier because I am still here physically to witness it.

Life can be short and every time I am able to laugh, exercise, walk, breathe, type, listen, see and be in this physical realm I am grateful.

I know I will meet my spirit family again, I just don't know when.

I don't want to force my mind back to the sad days anymore.

I have circled that ground for far too long.

I am thankful those times are far behind me.

But after all the deaths and all the people I have had to farewell, I realised we only *think* we have time, but time is not promised.

So, embrace this physical life as soon as you can.

The final word — Part 2

Your spirit folk want you to do as they did and live your life for all you are worth.

You have to grieve, it's true, but don't dwell on the sad days when happy days are happening now.

It is okay to let go of your grief. Letting go of your grief does not mean letting go of love for your spirit folk!

It means you are ready to embrace the simple fact their life was a gift to you.

They gave you all they had to give, and that is a beautiful and wonderful thing.

When you begin to enjoy life again, your spirit folk will be happy and excited to see you smile.

If you are not ready, you are not ready!

But never feel guilty for being ready to feel happy again.

This will take time, but I implore you to embrace this life while you can. Tomorrow is never promised.

Hug your people.

Call your people.

Eat with your people.

Laugh with your people.

Do this with them while you are all still physical.

Your spirit folk will wait, and they will understand if you are not always sad when you think of them. They prefer you to be happy when you think about the time they shared with you on Earth.

It's still early days for some of you. This message is not urging you to stop grieving but rather giving you hope that one day your new normal will be enough to make you happy again.

Live Life—Laugh Often—Love Always

CPSIA information can be obtained
at www.ICGtesting.com
Printed in the USA
LVHW020153281221
707246LV00003B/428

9 781925 846584